Awakening the Entrepreneurial Spirit in You!

Embracing Synchronicity

Dr. Pirjo Friedman, D.D.S.

PublishAmerica
Baltimore

First printing

ISBN: 1-4241-0738-5
PUBLISHED BY PUBLISHAMERICA, LLLP
www.publishamerica.com
Baltimore

Printed in the United States of America

Dear Anya,

Be the light and the love that you are!

Acknowledgements

"Life isn't about finding yourself. Life is about creating yourself."
George Bernard Shaw

As a dentist, the idea of writing a book was never at the top of my "to do" list. The inspiration first came to me during a consultation with a friend and futurist, Al Molyneaux. Throughout our sessions I would often share with Al my stories and experiences from various activities I was trying out. At one particular session I showed Al a stone on which the word "synchrodestiny" was engraved. While attuning to the energies of the stone as he held it in his hand, Al suddenly said, "You know, Pirjo, you could write a book about this." Al had planted the seed from which this book grew and he played an important role throughout the whole process by eagerly supporting me.

As soon as the idea to write the book sprang up, I got right to work. I wanted to tell the stories of synchronicities that have helped me shape my business and my life. I wanted to share these stories with others, highlighting the things that have guided me in my business with the hope they might help others as well.

With the help of my daughter, Kinneret, I began to record my stories for the book and she transcribed them to a word-processing document. After a short while I had countless stories, but it still wasn't a book.

At that time I was assisted by another friend, Ken Burgin. He was able to sort out the stories and knit them together into the existing form of this book. Ken was able to make what I wanted to say clear, without losing my own voice.

The final edit of the book was done by my daughter Shirrah, who managed to take the preliminary, raw version of the book, and mold it into a flowing and interesting read.

Other great contributors to the writing and inspiration of this book are my daughter, Tamar, who was my chief supporter every day throughout this lengthy process, though she often tells me to work less and get a life; Michael

Bazilinsky and Daniela Topali, two close friends who must have been truly tired of hearing my "progress reports" by the time the manuscript was completed; Miriam Sanua, who took over the book correspondence; and all the staff and associates of my office, Evelyn Racelis and Dr. Ceylanli in particular. Thank you to Yanka Van Der Kolk for the wonderful photos and Mercedeh Mohseni and Ken Burgin's creative ideas for developing the book cover.

You have all been an integral part of this book-writing process. Thank you for your inspiration and input!

Dr. Pirjo Friedman, D.D.S. 2005

Introduction

"Don't ask yourself what the world needs; ask yourself what makes you come alive. And then go and do that. Because what the world needs is people who have come alive."
Harold Whitman

Building a new business is tough for everyone, but I believe it is even more challenging for women. This is not because they are less capable than their male counterparts or possess lesser or weaker entrepreneurial skills, but rather because traditionally they are more involved in the day-to-day running and maintaining of the family home.

Women have been proving for the past few decades that it is possible to balance both a successful career and a thriving family life. How do they pull it off? Unfortunately, there is no text-book solution in this matter. Each woman must experiment, find her own path, and make it work for herself.

There is no shortage of self-help books listing what needs to be done in order to succeed and find happiness. This book does not recite the old recipe – work harder. I believe all you need to do is shift your consciousness just a little bit, transform your way of thinking to be positive. Then you can have it all. Anyone can do this by working in two realms, one physical and one spiritual.

My life, with all its aspects, is abundant. I am energized and healthy. I have a wonderful family and home as well as a successful business with remarkable employees. Let me show you how you can create all this with less effort, without spending every waking moment at the office.

There are many ways in which this can be done, and every person will find the methods which best work for them. I started by meditating and studying hypnosis, attending courses and seminars, reading books and applying what I learned from them. Your path may be different, but you need to start somewhere.

In this book, I wish to share with others the tools that have helped me create a joyful, no-stress life, while doing everything else at the same time: having a growing business, being an employer, finding solutions for financing, and ultimately doing less for more. Through sharing a series of stories from my life and career, I hope to demonstrate how you can deal with various challenging situations and how, through a shift of consciousness, the work that you do from within may enhance your experiences.

Take from this book as much as you can use or as little as you need.

"We learn more by looking for the answer to a question and not finding it than we do from learning the answer itself."

Lloyd Alexander

Chapter 1

Transformation —
Stocking Your Supermarket Cart

"What we see depends mainly on what we look for."
John Lubbock

At one time in my life I was commuting between Israel and Canada constantly, spending five weeks at a time in each destination. My former husband had accepted a position in Canada, and our three daughters and I joined him there. I had retained my practice in Israel for several years, as I was not licensed to practice dentistry in Canada, thus the commute. The hectic schedule played havoc with my life and relationship with my family.

My periods in Canada were composed mostly of free time. During the days, while my kids would be in school and my husband at work, I would look out the window thinking *Nobody lives here!* This was especially true during the long winters, as the streets were frozen and deserted.

After working full-time for years, I experienced space for the first time in my life. It seems we tend to busy ourselves with everyday life, leaving no room for change and transformation. During this period, however, frustrated with the excessive amount of free time, I became open to new ideas.

I was reading a book called *The Silva Method of Mind Control*, but though I found it interesting, I could not make any sense of it. *I cannot do this alone,* I thought. *I'd better find some help.*

I had never heard of the Silva Method before, and no one had ever mentioned it to me, so I didn't know where to go until I had a lunch meeting with a girlfriend in Jerusalem. The first thing I said to her was, "I have this book but..." Without waiting to hear the end of my sentence, this woman, who had never done any meditation before, said, "I have registered for a course called the *Silva Method of Mind Control* and it starts tomorrow." Needless to say, I also took the course. I stayed with my commitment to the Silva course until I felt that I had learned what I needed to know.

A similar scenario occurred with my interest in Kabbalah. During a conversation with a girlfriend, I happened to ask, "Do you know where I can study Kabbalah?" She replied, "Actually, I'm going to the Kabbalah Center right now." I went along with her. After having talked with the rabbi, it became important to me to study Kabbalah.

Generally speaking, I like to do things immediately when the thought occurs. I believe in the Buddhist saying, "When the student is ready, the master appears." That's the way it happened. Once again, I learned what I felt I needed. I found the lessons on astrology particularly interesting and I enjoyed meditating and spending Jewish holidays with the group. According to Kabbalistic teachings, the universe operates according to certain supremely powerful principles. By learning to understand and act in accordance with these principles, we can vastly improve our lives. With Kabbalah you transform and learn to become a sharing person. Once you become a sharing person, you find there is more energy available to you that you can channel from the universe to this earthly plane. It is a healing energy that you can draw upon to heal different parts of your life. The Kabbalah studies filled many gaps in my knowledge about different aspects of my life.

I continued my quest for learning. One day my husband's secretary mentioned that she was studying Reiki, and I asked her to tell me about it. I learned that Reiki is a technique for stress reduction and relaxation that allows anyone to tap into an unlimited supply of life force energy in the universe in order to improve health and enhance the quality of life. The knowledge that an unseen energy flows through all living things and is connected directly to the quality of health has existed since ancient times, and has been a part of the wisdom of many cultures.

The existence of this energy has long been verified by scientific experiments and many doctors now acknowledge its role in the proper functioning of the immune system and the great value it contributes to the healing process. Reiki treatments create a glowing radiance flowing through you and surrounding you. I immediately saw the correlation between Reiki and the Kabbalah, and before long I became a Reiki Master.

Next, I became interested in hypno-therapy and started reading all kinds of books about it. I located a hypnotist in the telephone book and called him, explaining that I wanted to study my past life.

"I'm sorry," he said "I don't deal with archaeology. I deal only with now and the future."

"Well, teach me what you can," I replied. "and I will use what I learn how I decide is best."

And that is what we did. I met with the hypnotist several times, during which I learned how to study more effectively. Fortunately, this was exactly the right thing for me to learn at the time, as I was about to take the examination that would allow me to practice dentistry in Canada.

In my daily meditations, I began to focus on how to pass my exam. The hypnotist had taught me how to perform self-hypnosis, which turned out to be of great help to focus my mind when I was studying. In retrospect, I wish I'd had that ability as a student in university, as I was never able to really sit down and concentrate on my studies. Since then twenty years has gone by during which I had not even tried to study. Instead, I would think about the lunch I needed to prepare, what I needed to shop for, when the kids would be home from school, or the spots on the kitchen floor. But now something had shifted and I changed. It became easy for me to study. I could sit and study for hours on end, forgetting about chores and everything else. It was amazing!

However, aside from being able to concentrate and study intensely, I was still worried about how I would do on the practical dentistry exam. I had been taking Kung Fu training for about fifteen years, and in a dream I saw myself sparring. I won every match, but while I was sparring, I was also teaching my opponent, coaching him on how to improve. I woke up thinking, *What am I worried about? I can do this! I know dentistry so well I can teach others about it!* Once I had completed the exams, I knew that I had passed. I did not have to wait for the results—I just knew!

My sparring dream came true, for soon after my exam I was offered a position at the university teaching other foreign dentists how to study for the exam. This was a hands-on, practical course on materials and dentistry. Of all the instructors of the course, I was the only one that had actually taken the exam; the others were all grad students who had studied in Canada. For that reason, my students could really identify with me and I could relate to them. Aside from teaching dentistry, I also coached them on how to mentally prepare for the exam.

Some of the students I taught were very stressed. I often heard them complain, "I can't sleep, I'm a wreck, I'm falling to pieces." I would frequently invite them to my office for a Reiki treatment. One student told me she was so stressed that she was not able to sleep. When she came to the office I simply gave her a hug. Later she said, "I don't know how it happened, but the moment you hugged me I felt energy. It was as though something was lifted off my shoulders. I went home and slept for twelve hours. I feel so much better!"

I was as amazed as she was about the results, if not more so. These experiences were teaching me about energy exchange between people. I realized that when used in dentistry, Reiki can be a natural tool to promote relaxation of the body as well as calm feelings of anxiety. I began to see the potential of using Reiki as a method of boosting my dental practice, and that is exactly what I started to do. I soon began receiving feedback from patients telling me that Reiki provides them with a sense of peace, security, and well-being that makes their dental visit a more pleasant experience than they ever expected. Some say they actually feel better after the dental treatment than they did before they came in!

I always compare learning to shopping. When you go to the supermarket you see that everybody has different items in their carts. The same applies to learning. When you attend courses, read books or listen to tapes, it is just like shopping. You don't need to take everything. You only take what you think you need and what you feel is good and useful. You always know what is best for you.

Chapter 2
Synchronicity — It's All Around You

*"There are no mistakes, no coincidences. All events are blessings
given to us to learn from."*
Elisabeth Kubler-Ross

About six years ago, I attended a course given by Deepak Chopra. It was his inaugural course on "synchrodestiny," the term he had coined for the parts of synchronicity that are concerned with charting one's future. Synchronicity was a subject that I was very interested in learning more about as I had been experiencing a lot of it.

The twenty-five attendants, including myself, convened in LaJolla, California, and during four days performed a variety of practical exercises. The theme and purpose of the workshop was to understand synchrodestiny— a coming together of seemingly unrelated events *that may affect one's life course in the future*. It was not long before we realized that synchronicity had already existed among us, and we all seemed to be connected by a variety of events. For example, although the attendants had all arrived from assorted places worldwide, we discovered that many of us knew other people in common. I was intrigued.

Before I continue recapping my first synchrodestiny experience, I would like to retreat a little further to the time I first got involved with Deepak Chopra's teachings. In retrospect, it seems that numerous separate paths have led me to him. At the beginning of the 1990s I found myself examining a particular book repeatedly in a Toronto bookstore—a book written by Deepak Chopra. The back of the book included Chopra's picture, and although I was unfamiliar with him at the time, I felt compelled by his photograph. It so happened that a few months later I received an audiotape by Deepak Chopra from a friend. Although it took me nearly a year to get around to listening to the tape, once I had I could not resist listening to it daily, enjoying the inspired words of healing for the body and the mind.

Shortly thereafter, while having lunch with a friend, I learned that she was planning to attend one of Deepak Chopra's lectures. I decided to join her, as I had been noticing the synchronicity around me for some time now.

Chopra's teachings immediately captured my attention and interest. He spoke of coincidences, referring to them as *The Conspiracy of Improbabilities* and the importance of being conscious of them. I left the meeting fascinated and eager to learn as much as possible.

Following that eye-opening experience, I began to notice the synchronicities surrounding me more than ever before. I became aware of the simplest coincidences marking my path. For instance, I'd be driving and thinking of a file where I keep alternative healthcare tips and articles for my patients to browse through in the waiting room of my office. I was considering having my daughter make a cover with a "smiley face" for the file. Moments later, I was driving past a huge smiley face sign by the side of the road.

Another day, while reflecting on a car I was considering buying, the very same car, model and color I wanted to buy drove up beside me.

Once, on my way to the Four Seasons Hotel, I hailed a taxi and as I was instructing the driver where to go, I noticed a store named "Four Seasons" outside the window.

Another time, while driving to the airport to meet a business associate, I was having second thoughts about whether the meeting was a good idea or not. While entertaining my doubts, I suddenly noticed three consecutive cars, all of which had the same letters on their license plates: "YOB." While in past years I probably would not have noticed such a coincidence, let alone give it meaning, I decided it must be a sign I was doing the right thing. Ever since then, any time I have had doubts or reservations about something, I remember that experience and search for a clue. Amazingly, I have noticed that often when I would be deliberating on some subject while driving, I would see that same license plate with the letters "YOB," and consider it a confirmation. You cannot force a sign to appear, but if you are open to receiving it, an answer will often arise.

I was out walking one afternoon and my cell phone rang. It was a friend calling from Europe. She had been to visit me the week before and she had seen something in a store here that she had wanted to buy but had not gotten around to before she had to leave. She asked if I could go to that store and pick up the article for her. I said, "That will not be a problem as I am standing outside that very store as we speak!"

One day, I had a new patient in my dental chair and we were making small talk. He was a university student from Japan and I happened to mention a new picture book I had just bought about water crystals. The book was from Japan and the text was half in Japanese. I suggested he might be interested in seeing it as he could actually read the text. Surprisingly he said, "Not only can I read the text, but the thesis I am writing is on crystals and I would be more than interested!" I had never met the man before and I had no idea about his thesis being on something as obscure as water crystals.

Not long after my first Deepak Chopra meeting, as I became increasingly aware of the synchronicity around me, I decided I wanted to learn more. I signed up for a three-day course in Toronto called *The Journey into the Boundless*, led by Deepak Chopra. Once again it proved a worthwhile experience. Next, I attended Chopra's seven-day course called *Seduction of the Spirit*. This course took place in Ghoa, India, and included several hours of meditation each day, followed by workshops. It was there when I learned the benefits of daily meditation, and I have been doing it religiously ever since.

Following these events, I attended Chopra's first-ever Synchrodestiny course at the Deepak Chopra Center in LaJolla, California, topped by a trip to Egypt, led by Chopra, Wayne Dyer and Laura Day. This week-long journey included a group of nearly a hundred people from different places worldwide, cruising the Nile and meditating at ancient temples, the Pyramids, and other places characterized by high energies.

By this time I was completely fascinated by the subject. I look back at these events as steps of initiation, improving my awareness and understanding of what was surrounding me. In my search for further knowledge and perspectives I also became involved with hypnosis and Kabbalah, the Jewish mysticism. At one point, while sharing my experiences with a rabbi, he encouraged me, saying, "Your guides in the spirit realm want to talk to you. They want to help. You probably have some purpose and goals that you are working on and they are just trying to get your attention. Start connecting and talking to them."

The rabbi continued to explain that people make choices, with which the guides in the spirit realm cannot interfere. Therefore, unless we ask for it, they cannot provide us with direction. The rabbi compared this to a phone call—you can either make the call or choose not to. However, unless you call, you will not be connected.

I took the rabbi's advice to mind and began using my free time, usually while driving, to "connect" with my spirit guides. I eventually developed a private joke, and whenever I was planning something, I would say, "Thanks for helping me. We're a team, let's do this together!"

Meanwhile, incidents of synchronicity continued to occur. For example, one of my patients is a fashion designer, and has tailored some business suits for me in the past. One morning, I decided it was time to order two new suits. Luckily when I arrived at work I noticed her name on that day's schedule. When she came in for her appointment, we spoke about the fabric, color, and style of the new suit. Later that week I received a visit from another longtime friend who has also made some outfits for me in the past. The reason for her visit was to tell me about some fabrics she had bought with me in mind. As it turned out, not only were the fabrics exactly the same as the ones I had ordered from the other designer, they were already cut to suit the style I sought. Since the opportunity had presented itself, I decided to make room in my closet for four new suits!

Unfortunately, when I spoke with the first designer the following week, I learned that she would not be able to make the suits due to some personal problems. By then, however, my friend had completed my suits, which were precisely what I intended to get in the first place! In retrospect, I realized that although I had requested something from one person who was not able to fulfill it, another person had, neither of them knowing about the other. It was synchronicity.

Over the years I learned how remarkable synchronicity is, but mostly I was fascinated by its simplicity. The trick is to allow room for things to happen—accept them, rather than fight them. Do not waste energy on worrying, fretting, or trying to control everything. If something doesn't happen, let it go. Sometimes you must wait. Be open and aware to messages around you, signs presenting answers to your questions. However, you *must* ask the questions. Everybody and everything can become a messenger for you, as you could be for others.

One day I was out walking with one of my daughters and I came upon a woman who was just beginning to pack up the yard sale she'd been having. I noticed a lot of beautiful baby clothes and as I was admiring them the woman said, "Why don't you just take them off my hands?" Although I had no need for them, I did just that and it so happened that the next person I spoke with that evening told me she was helping out a young mother of a newborn baby and she needed baby clothes. I was glad to be able to pass them on! It was almost as if someone had been putting out a request for baby clothes and somehow I was part of the answer.

Another time, I had this expensive inhaler that my daughter had needed when we lived in Israel. When we moved to Canada, however, it was left in storage in Israel. One day, during one of my stays in Israel, I decided I would pass the inhaler on to my daughter's former pediatrician. I happened to mention this to my first patient that day who, as it turned out, was the pediatrician's receptionist! When she left my office, she happily took the inhaler with her.

On yet another occasion, I was flying to a conference in Washington where I was to deliver a short speech. I was concerned because I felt my speech lacked a strong closing. I was reading one of Deepak Chopra's books and I had just read something he said about luck being "opportunity and preparedness coming together." As I thought about that, I put down the book and began thumbing through an airline magazine. The pages fell open at an article about a businessman who had built a successful chain of small luxury hotels. His advice almost leaped off the page at me — he said, "Luck is preparedness meeting opportunity." He may have been quoting Deepak Chopra, but the message was clear: I should use that sentence to close my speech in Washington.

These are examples of synchronicity and I am convinced everyone has experienced similar occurrences—the person that just happens to be on the phone as you lift the receiver to call them; the song you were thinking of that just happens to be playing on the radio when you turn it on. In fact, I had something like that happen to me recently. In the clinic, we keep twenty-five music CDs on the play list. Generally we have the player switched to random so we never know what will play next. One day, one of my staff happened to notice that Ravel's "Bolero" was coming up too often and we all had "Bolero" reverberating in our brains. I removed the CDs and mixed them up before reinstalling them. When I switched the system on, the first piece played was "Bolero." But that's not all, when I turned on the radio in my car that day, what was playing? You guessed it—"Bolero"! Was this a message of some kind?

Sometimes, when you are in tune with your surroundings, people may communicate although no words are spoken. For instance, more than once I have been able to know when a person is pregnant even in the very early stages of the pregnancy.

A few months ago, I had a patient come in who I knew was suffering from Crohn's disease. I had just heard about a natural supplement that is very effective at relieving the symptoms. I wanted to recommend it to her but I felt uncomfortable raising the subject. On her next visit, I noticed that the patient looked radiantly healthy. When I commented about it, she told me that she had taken away a free health magazine the last time she had been in our office, and noticed an advertisement for that same supplement I was thinking of telling her about!

In Israel, I had known some of my patients for as long as twenty years, and they trusted and respected me. Occasionally when a patient would come in, I could feel that something was wrong and I would ask them what the problem was. On one occasion a patient confided in me, saying, "I don't know what to do. I want to become a graphic designer, but I am not sure if it is the right profession for me."

My response was, "I believe you can change your profession four times in your lifetime. It's not a big deal. Go and study!"

A year later that patient returned, saying, "You don't know how much you helped me that day!" By then, she had received positive feedback that she had made the right decision. Our short conversation provided that patient with the positive sign she needed to make her decision. It was her bit of synchrodestiny.

The moment I passed the dentistry exam in Canada, I wanted to buy my own dental practice. I tend not to be very patient with the searching process for too long, which I prefer to see as spontaneity. I belong to the "I want it now!" school of thought and therefore did not envisage going to many practices, analyzing charts and financial statements, and so on. Luckily for me, synchronicity occurred once again. A friend informed me that he knew a dentist, Dr. Ceylanli, who was interested in selling his practice. He asked if I was interested. Naturally, I said I was.

The rest happened quickly: I went there, agreed on a price, we shook hands, and the deal was made. I never checked a single thing. I relied on my trust and intuition, and Dr. Ceylanli has been the best thing that could ever happen to me. Dr. Ceylanli told me once that I would never regret knowing him, and he was right. To this day he loves to come to the office, and we love having him there. He is now over eighty years old and is there almost every day. We help each other out in every possible way. In my case, acquiring an office was all a matter of knowing what is right when it appeared. But to be able to know what is right, you have to know what you are looking for. Once you have that covered, you will be presented with the right solution.

Even at times when the options you are presented with do not seem like the correct solutions to your problem, trust that your creativity can make the difference. In fact, there aren't any wrong decisions to be made! My resolution to purchase Dr. Ceylanli's practice could have turned out to be the wrong one, but I could sense the potential and I was determined to commit to the effort and make it successful. I did not let the initial challenges discourage me.

When you purchase a dental practice, you acquire a patient list as well as the equipment. My purchase included a very modest list of patients, of which only half remained my patients. The ones who continued coming, however, were very good patients.

I will never forget my first day at the new practice. Two of Dr. Ceylanli's patients had agreed to come and see me. In the morning, when I arrived at the clinic, Dr. Ceylanli had a long face. "I've got really bad news," he said "the first patient died last night, and the second patient got in a car accident because of a snowstorm and broke his arm on the way here!"

The news was devastating to me, but I knew I had to keep a positive attitude, despite the unfortunate turn of events. I made a mental note to keep in mind that the patient who had died was eighty-six years old, so it was obviously his time. The other patient came in at a later date with his arm in a sling. It is always wise to keep a sense of humor. Despite the discouraging start, I made a mental note that as soon as possible, I had to get out there and start building my own list of patients, using every means humanly possible.

By this time you may have noticed the extent synchronicity was playing a role in my life and the power it had in guiding me through everything I did. As I became more and more aware of the part synchronicity was playing, I became increasingly willing to trust the messages that came my way. Even during difficult situations—throughout my divorce, taking the national board exam and starting my business—I felt like I was never alone. All the clues were there for me to find—little signs waiting to guide and help me. It was encouraging.

Synchronicities are the clues that help us answer the questions that we put out into the universe. If you are aware of what you are asking for and keep yourself open to the clues that are all around, making decisions will become easier.

Chapter 3
Manifesting — Picturing Your Success

"Imagination is the beginning of creation.
You imagine what you desire, you will what you imagine,
and at last you create what you will."
George Bernard Shaw

How do you know which way to go if you have no idea where you want to get to? In business it is said that in order to set a direction and achieve certain objectives, one must first formulate a general idea of where they would like to see their business in the future. The strategy of a business therefore includes a final goal, which outlines the direction the business must take in order to achieve this vision. The same is true for life in general. The business community would call this process strategizing; I refer to it as manifesting. Simply put, manifesting is picturing what you want to achieve, and keeping it in mind every step of the way. When I first started my career, I envisioned myself running a successful practice in a pleasant office, surrounded by first-rate staff and many patients. I have kept this image in my mind for many years, and ensured that every move or decision I made regarding my practice was inline with this vision. Eventually my foresight became a reality.

Manifesting works in a general, broad manner, as well as with small matters. It is a "two-way street," meaning you can send signals regarding your own manifestations as well as receive others'. My office manager, Daniela, and I have been working together for several years and have developed an intense understanding between us, a mental connection even. This has lead to several instances of near telepathic communication. For example, one morning I arrived at the office and told her that I thought it was time to give her a raise. She laughed and said, "Wow, I was thinking yesterday about asking for one!" It seems I somehow sensed her wish and by recognizing it, I could help her manifest her aspiration. This is an example of how manifesting one's goal, large or small, is transmitted into the world, by that allowing it to become a reality.

It is important to realize, however, that while you can manifest your ambitions, you cannot force them to realize. The trick is to focus on your goal and at the same time release control of the process. Enjoy the moment and trust that whatever happens is in your best interest. Moreover, remember that the universe is more willing to support you when you are helping others to succeed.

During my journey to India for the Deepak Chopra conference, I was so busy with the rigorous conference agenda that I only realized on my last day that I hadn't had time for any souvenir and gift shopping for my family. My return trip included an overnight stay in Bombay, though by the time I arrived there, all stores were closed. As I was standing with my suitcases in the lobby of my hotel in Bombay, a woman approached me and asked if I'd like to do some shopping. It turned out that she owned a souvenir store in the hotel, and although she had already closed for the night, she was willing to open the store again. Astonished at the rare opportunity, I immediately took her up on the offer.

On another occasion I was visiting my family in Finland. During one of the family gatherings I met my cousin who had a small golden heart glued onto one of her front teeth. The ornament was charming and unique and I decided to offer similar jewelry in my office. The next morning I was looking for a place to have a broken travel bag repaired. I remembered a little store in town that provided shoe repair service, but when I arrived there it turned out to be a brand new jewelry store! I asked the owner about the little gold figures for tooth jewelry, mentioning I would only be in the country for a few more days. As I was the first customer and the owner was very eager for business, he fulfilled my wish. Once again I got what I had been wishing for, and returned home with a variety of lovely golden tooth jewelry.

In my practice I often use a curing lamp to harden some of the materials I work with, particularly the material used for tooth-colored fillings. While I was still working in Israel, I made use of a lamp that was about fifteen years old. Although the lamp had never given me any problems, one day I mentioned to my assistant that we should look into buying a new lamp. After inquiring with the dental supply, we decided to abandon the idea, as the price we were quoted was very high. The very next day, however, while I was using the lamp, it suddenly sputtered and died. As my work was mostly restorations and tooth-colored fillings, it was essential that I have a lamp urgently. My assistant called the dental depot once again and was told that although they usually order-in these items from another location, they just happened to get one that day, and would be able to supply it to us in a matter of minutes. This was exceptionally good timing, as I would have had to cancel all my patients otherwise. I found out later that the reason the dental supply office had the lamp on hand was because we had called them to inquire about it the day before. They decided that they should order a lamp just in case one was needed. My seemingly unfounded initial concern about the lamp appears to have caused a series of events that created a positive outcome.

The events surrounding the lamp were peculiar but I had not thought much about it while it was happening. Later, however, I became intrigued, thinking, *What is going on?* By that time, I was aware of synchronistic events taking place, but I was growing increasingly puzzled by the causes for their occurrence. I decided to consult with a friend who read futures.

At the session, after discussing my goals and aspirations in life, he hypnotized me. While under hypnosis, my friend suggested various scenarios that I had described as optimal life situations earlier. Afterwards, he assisted me in writing out my goals on piece of paper, which I was to copy out every night for a period of thirty days, before going to bed. This turned out to be an effective device in keeping my focus on my manifestation. In a month, I was a great deal more confident of my goals, and by focusing on them 24/7, I began seeing things coming together to materialize them.

Do not be fooled—manifestation did not make my goals materialize magically. However, as my mind became clearer as to what I wanted and where I wanted to be, manifesting became easier. When you envision your goals clearly and dispose of unnecessary, negative and contradicting thoughts from your mind, the likelihood of achieving your goals will multiply.

Chapter 4
Positive Thinking —
You Are What You Think

"Optimism is the faith that leads to achievement. Nothing can be done without hope and confidence."
Helen Keller

I often hear people say, "I have no time!" If this sounds familiar, you may consider changing your attitude, since time is limitless. We artificially fragment time into bits and pieces, to our detriment. Some people tend to shorten or tighten time in their minds since they really believe that there is not enough time, thus creating stress for themselves. Although it is nice to be on time, the fact is that it is not always possible. Countless reasons may cause us to be late, sometimes beyond our control.

One of the first rules I have made for myself quite early in my life was never to worry about being late until the exact time of the appointment. In my experience, if I do not worry, more often than not things just seem to work out—the other person may also be late, for example. Concept of time is individual, but one thing is for sure: not worrying about it sure eliminates a lot of stress!

Try thinking, *I always have enough time for everything I need to do.* Time will seemingly stretch and you will stay calm.

When you are anxious, nothing seems to flow properly. Matters that would otherwise come easily become strenuous. You may forget details because your mind is congested. You become entangled in a web of fretting, thinking *Nothing is going my way!* Thinking this way will eventually manifest that exact scenario. It has been said, "In the province of the mind, what one believes to be true, either is true or becomes true."

This is the energy of thought. Keep it positive. Think, *I have enough time, I have everything I need, I remember everything I need at the right time,* and so on. This thinking will generate a shift of consciousness. The way you think and the words you use will determine the outcome.

My National Board dentistry exams lasted five days and were potentially very stressful. During this time I meditated daily about how grateful I was. I kept repeating to myself, *I have everything I need: the knowledge, the equipment, the skills. It is easy for me, and I enjoy it.* And I did enjoy it! Following the exams, I was approached by few people who claimed I actually looked like I was having fun during the exam! By maintaining a positive outlook, the whole ordeal became amazingly easy for me.

Success does not have to mean hard work or giving up enjoying your children, life, holidays, or an intimate relationship. Although building a successful business can become a burden, it does not have to be. If you feel that you have to spend every waking moment at the business your life will suffer. The first things to go are usually intimacy and the relationship you have with your children. Next follow the guilt and stress. The longer you remain in this destructive cycle the more you exhaust yourself. You may think the only solution is to give up something, but this is not true. The truth is that you can continue working and balancing your relationships successfully by simply altering your internal "software."

Life becomes difficult when you spend your energy fighting and resenting it. Your negativity makes being difficult. Surprisingly, in order to thrive, it is not necessary to work harder. More precisely, it is not necessary to find the work hard—you should enjoy what you do, or as Willie Hill put it, "Once you do something you love, you never have to work again."

Do not create stress for yourself by concentrating on negativity or worrying about failure. Relax and benefit by knowing you will be successful. Keeping a positive attitude will help you far more than worrying ever will.

Chapter 5

Getting Business —
The Power of Networking and
Word of Mouth

*"Ordinary people can spread good and bad information about
brands faster than marketers."*
Ray Johnson

When I first bought my clinic in Toronto, I also acquired the previous owner's patient list. Although the list contained many good patients at the time, I realized that it was still not enough to build the thriving and profitable practice I intended. By that time I had been practicing dentistry for twenty years and had developed my experience through hard work and exertion. I wanted to create a winning practice promptly. Working another straining twenty years was not what I had in mind.

During the first few months of operation, business was very slow ,with only few patients coming in every week. On the other hand, I had loan payments and office expenses to disburse, causing endless sleepless nights of concern and anxiety. I soon realized that the situation could continue in this fashion, and that I must take every possible measure to attract patients and promote my business.

The first steps I took were traditional marketing activities, such as placing ads in various publications and launching a website. The most effective method I found, however, was *networking*. Joining nearly every club and organization listed, I would go out every night for networking meetings, introducing myself to a large variety of people and handing out my business card. As a matter of fact, during my first year of business I gave away over one thousand business cards!

Although my life had become quite strenuous during these months, juggling my family, work at the clinic and efforts to build up my patient list, my pains soon bore fruit and my networking was paying off by supplying an increasing flow of new patients whom I had met personally or who were referred to me.

Working as a dentist can be extremely arduous on the body, and over the years I learned the value of preserving my health and well-being through an assortment of therapies. Besides my weekly massage, I believe and benefit from shiatsu, acupuncture, homeopathy, reflexology, and NLP to name but a few. I enjoy experiencing a little of everything, a quality which I believe contributed greatly to my success, as well as to my networking. By becoming a client of other healthcare practitioners, I often obtain them as my clients in return. As we get to know each other and become confident about each other's skills, we begin to refer patients to one another. In fact, I use my office itself for networking, displaying their business cards in my waiting room.

Although networking is a very demanding method at first, it becomes less time-consuming after a while. Now that I have built a practice with a significant number of patients, they provide me with new patients regularly by word-of-mouth referrals. The era of sleepless nights is over, which enables me to relax and relate to experiences and occurrences around me. Most importantly, it allows me to remain aware of the messages and signals that are there for me if I care to listen—more synchronicity.

Apparently, synchronicity comes into play quite frequently in word-of-mouth interactions. For example, one day we were expecting a new patient named Sarah. During the same time, a woman walked into the clinic, took a brief look around and walked back out. Daniela, my office manager, assumed the woman was the new patient and was concerned about why she had left the office. She caught up to the woman in the corridor and asked her if she was Sarah. Astounded, the woman answered, "Yes, I am Sarah." It turned out, however, that this woman was not the same Sarah who had booked the appointment. This woman had been shopping around for a new dentist and had apparently gotten off the elevator at the wrong floor, spotted my office door, and decided to take a look on a whim. Convinced by the astonishing coincidence, the new Sarah booked an appointment, and is a patient of mine to this day, even though she has since moved to the United States.

As peculiar as the whole incident was, it was not synchronicity's final role in the story. A few weeks later Sarah had been on her way to see a spiritual healer who practices in my building. While talking with the healer, Sarah showed him my business card and said, "Here's a good dentist if you ever need one." The healer took my card, and as it so happened, his next patient, Esther, arrived with a severe toothache. He gave her my business card, saying, "You should go see this dentist. She is just downstairs, and I hear she's good."

Coincidentally, as Esther was leaving his office, she met another woman in the waiting room, who, noticing her grasping her cheek, offered to recommend her a good dentist in the building—me!

Thanks to synchronicity I gained two new patients at once, and they, in turn, have referred others.

Another time, one of my patients told me that he had taken a training course and during a break in one of the sessions, he began telling his classmates about his dentist who was also a Reiki master. Out of the fourteen people in his class, it turned out that several were already my patients. He was astonished, to say the least! This story is an example of the true power of word-of-mouth referrals, with an added dose of synchronicity.

Another example is the story of the family who has just moved to the city. When the father of the family began looking for a good dentist, he was referred to me by his daughter's orthodontist as well as by the priest in his church, both of whom did not know each other. I remember being completely surprised at how two unrelated people, in a city of millions, had referred the same dentist!

I once attended a meeting and was approached by a woman who said, "I've been looking forward to meeting you!" It turned out that a friend of her's, who is a patient of mine, had recommended me and given her my card. Several days later, she had met a neighbor of mine who had also recommended me. Next she attended the meeting and there I was!

Another time, I had invited a new member of the Women Entrepreneurs over for dinner. She asked if she could bring a friend along and I agreed. When they came to my door, I was surprised to see that her friend was a patient of mine. That patient told me later that on the way up the elevator, she had been telling the other woman about her dentist and recommending me. She did not know it was me that they were coming to see!

You can easily see how my networking was paying off. I was out to get patients and was constantly meeting people. I was also manifesting my desire for more patients. When you know your goals and you focus on them, synchronicity kicks in.

I still advertise in the traditional marketing channels. However, there are other ways. I've had a web site for a few years, but it wasn't getting much traffic. At one of the times when I was thinking, *I need more patients, how do I do this?*, someone I was talking to mentioned that the Women Entrepreneurs website is now at the top of search engine results. "Which engine?" I asked. "How can I do that?" They explained it to me, and I went to my web designer and asked him to make the same changes. Since then my site has been getting more and more hits every month. A far cry from the eleven I had a year ago!

When it comes to advertising, my advice is to market your business in the right channels, but make sure you advertise in the "universe" as well. You will have your spiritual guides working there for you full-time. You can also do as I do with my patients and say, "We'd love to have more patients like you. If you like our service, please tell your friends and family." It may happen that the next person they encounter will be searching for the same service you provide.

Chapter 6

Financing—It May Be Right under Your Nose

"Money doesn't bring happiness and creativity.
Your creativity and happiness bring money."
Sam Rosen

During the years I was commuting between Canada and Israel, I experienced high fixed costs as my office in Jerusalem was leased and I was paying rent during the weeks I spent in Toronto, as well as the salary of my assistant, as she was taking care of business and office maintenance in my absence.

One day, while I was in Canada, my assistant in Israel phoned to let me know that the bank was no longer honoring my checks due to high debt. The situation had confirmed my suspicions—that costs were too high and revenues too low. Bouncing checks had raised the situation to an alarming state.

With high expenses on both sides of the world and business still very slow in Toronto, I did not know where to start looking for funds. The state of emergency forced me to go to Israel at once in order to figure out a way to wipe out my debts.

In two days I was back in my Jerusalem clinic, working around the clock. I had a deadline to work by, as I had a return flight to Canada in two weeks. A few days before my flight back it was becoming painfully obvious that the crisis was far from being over and I would have to find new ways to cut costs and increase revenue. After studying the books for a while, my assistant mentioned an old bank account I had kept for many years, but rarely used. The only activities in this account were the periodic fees I was paying. "By closing this account," she said, "you will have one less expense to cover. It may not be much, but it's something."

The first chance I got, I went to the bank with the intention of closing the account. While doing this, the manager asked me what I wanted to do with the pension plan that I had there. It turned out that I had been making automatic contributions to this pension fund for over fifteen years and I had completely forgotten about it. Luckily, the plan had just become available for redemption the week before and had enough money to pay off all my bills and more!

Once again, I was amazed at how well everything worked out—a financial calamity had turned out for the best. I decided to let this incident be a lesson for me, realizing that every situation is positive if only you approach it from the right perspective. In retrospect, I realized that if I had stayed and tried to solve the problem from Toronto, waiting for the one and a half patients I had per week, I would have made myself sick with worry, while my business would probably have worsened. The most important insight was that the solution was right under my nose. All I had to do was be aware and seek it.

With the money I uncovered from the pension account, I was finally able to close the practice in Jerusalem and put an end to the stressful commuting, concentrating on my new practice in Toronto.

I believe the most important and fundamental key to success in anything, whether in business or in one's personal life, is to remain positive, since negativity has a tendency to create obstacles. This includes leading a way of life devoid of negativity, which may be different from one person to another. I, for example, rarely ever read or watch the media, particularly the news, since I do not wish to focus on disaster. Instead, I focus on removing all things and aspects of my life that do not contribute to my well-being. I am positive that whatever I need to know, I will find out some way or other, while filtering all other negative information that clutters the news. I strongly believe that I am a happier and more positive person thanks to this, and that this has greatly contributed to my success.

The same positive attitude applies to finance. When I first started investing in my business, it was clear that my finances were insufficient. I would often have nightmares about exceeding my overdraft limit. Gradually, I became more financially secure, and I could finally afford to spend a little, renovating the clinic and investing in expanding my patient list. Although those investments lowered my bank balance to just above the line once again, I felt confident in my choices. As the saying goes: "you have to spend money to make money." Although it is a risky business, you have to trust your instincts that what you are doing is right for you, and that everything will work out for the best. Even when things do not work out the way you expected them to—all you can do is accept them and do anything in your power to set them right.

If you are not happy with your accountant or your banker, trust your instincts and replace them. Honor yourself, honor your feelings, and make a change. Changing an accountant or bank may be a hassle and time consuming, but it can be done, and if you feel this is what needs to be done it will be worth your while. By remaining positive and trusting your gut, proceeding step-by-step, before you know it, you will be in a different situation, a better situation, and it will all be worth it. Do not worry about the apparent indecisiveness and lack of stability of repeatedly changing banks, like many other things it is a learning experience, aimed at finding the one service that fits your purposes best. I have changed banks frequently, looking for new financial sources and never satisfied with the line of credit I received. In fact, only recently I have once again changed banks, and although it hasn't been long, I have a feeling that this one will stick. Finally, after transferring and trying on the services of many banks, I have found the one that best complements and benefits my business.

It seems that banks all have one thing in common: when you are in really tough situations and you need them the most, they cannot, or *will* not, help you. There were times when I was in challenging financial circumstances, and although I do not recommend that anybody work so close to disaster, if you do find yourself in these thorny conditions, you must trust that it is all going to work itself out somehow. However, it is your responsibility to be aware and search for solutions. For example, there was one point when I desperately needed funding and miraculously, I found one bank that did come to my rescue. While searching for banks that would extend my line of credit, a friend advised me to call a bank that was offering credit simply by phoning. I called right away and in less than fifteen minutes on the phone, the bank gave me a $25,000 line immediately!

Time and money are similar concepts in the sense that they are both very much a state of mind. I mentioned earlier the common saying "you have to spend money to make money." I believe this saying could be approached from another perspective: you have to *think* money to make money.

Obsessing about finances that you need, but do not have, will never "show you the money." On the other hand, believing the funds are always there for you to find is guaranteed to put you on the right track. Next time you feel you need a little boost in your financial situation, try a trick I learned from a friend.

A few years ago, I was in New York, visiting this friend, who has a great wealth of knowledge in new age subjects: past life, hypnosis, and so on. I spent a couple of days with her to learn from her expertise. As we talked, the subject of money and achieving wealth came up. Part of her advice, as strange as it may sound, was to go to a bank and request brand new money. Take it home and smell it, roll on it, have fun with it! I thought she must be joking. A few days later, however, I happened to be using a bank machine, and low and behold, I received a stack of new fifty-dollar bills! It was the first time that I had ever gotten fifty-dollar bills from the machine, until that day the bank machines only supplied twenty-dollar bills. I decided to keep these bills separate from the money I was about to spend. The very next day, as I was preparing to go on another short trip to the U.S., I exchanged some currency for American dollars. Imagine my surprise when the teller handed me several brand new hundred-dollar bills!

To conclude, finances should not always be approached "by the book." Sometimes a more relaxed and unorthodox approach may be useful. More often than not, when you have exhausted all the traditional ways of financing, the money you need may be found in the strangest and most extraordinary places, in line with your needs. All you have to do is keep an open mind!

Chapter 7
Staffing — The Power of First Impressions

"Strength lies in differences, not in similarities."
Stephen Covey

I have built my office in way that provides a harmonious environment, where my employees may be content and peaceful in their work and where patients can unwind and even enjoy their treatment. This atmosphere, much like Rome, was not built in a day, however, and required a series of staffing decisions and relationships that evolved over time.

When I first purchased the clinic from Dr. Ceylanli, there was only the two of us. He was with me during that first devastating day and to this day continues to be my mentor, friend, and handyman. But once I was able to build up a list of regular patients and the practice began to gain momentum, I needed to expand my staff. Over the years I have managed to compose a diverse office, full of superb and brilliant individuals.

Although I have mostly made wise employment decisions, the process of recruiting and developing human resources is a complicated and tricky business, and is often risky. My office, as any other business, has suffered some challenges associated with the staff. There have been a few members of my team who have tested my goodwill and hindered the flow and profitability of the business by not showing up to work when I wasn't there or neglecting to fulfill their responsibilities on time. The most important thing in these situations is to learn from past mistakes and do whatever you can to improve them. For example, during the first year, I had employed a receptionist who had led the office to near crisis by forgetting to pay various bills. It so happened, that during that same time, my eldest daughter had come home from Israel for several months. She was in need of a job, and as I could no longer trust my employee, I had let her go and hired my daughter instead.

Before long, in addition to Dr. Ceylanli, my office was becoming a family enterprise, with my eldest daughter in charge of the reception and bookkeeping, my middle daughter deciphering the technical instruction manuals of all the equipment and appliances in the office, and my youngest daughter tagging along for joy and entertainment. With everybody's help, I could finally take control of the practice and concentrate on building it further.

Eventually, my practice expanded and with my daughter returning to Israel, the need arose for a full-time office manager. Once again, in line with my need, came the solution. During this time I went to a party of friends and met Daniela. She had been working in a clinic as a replacement for someone who was on maternity leave, but who was expected to return soon. I learned that she was a medical doctor, educated in Europe, and therefore was a little concerned that she may find it unsatisfying to work as a dental office receptionist. However, she called me up the day after the party and said, "I want to work with you. Pay me what you can afford, and if you think I'm good, you can upgrade my salary as we go." She started working the following week.

Daniela understood that my financial situation was rough at the time, but she sensed the potential of the business and put her faith in it. Daniela joining my team has proved to be the best thing for both of us in the long run.

The recruiting and hiring process can be a complex one, which I try to circumvent by relying mostly on my gut and intuition. Although interviews are claimed to be the hiring tool with the highest chances of predicting success, I do not like to spend a lot of time reading resumes, since it is time consuming and drives me away from other things I'd rather be doing, such as looking after my patients. However, when you place an ad in the help wanted section of the newspaper, resumes are what you get. In my experience, I've found that referrals from people you trust are always the best method of recruiting, although there are other ways of course. And while other people may choose to interview as many candidates as possible before making a decision, I wait until my instincts indicate someone—which may well be the first person I've interviewed!

When I needed to hire a chair-side assistant, it was surprisingly simple and painless. I had advertised the position in the newspaper and received over twenty resumes. Evelyn, who has graduated as a dentist in the Philippines and worked as an assistant in the Middle East for fifteen years, was the first applicant I interviewed and I employed her on the spot. She started work as early as the next day, and has been with me ever since. Straight off I felt comfortable working with her, and I feel we are very much in sync. Once again, I trusted my instincts and it couldn't have worked out better!

A few years ago I first met someone who has what I call "intuitions." She works for various companies, helping them choose the right employees by examining candidates' resumes. "I hope they never find out how I do it, as they are under the impression I actually do research," she says. "What I do is simply spread the papers out on a table and put my hand on top of them. If my hand gets hot, it's a good applicant. If it gets cold, that applicant should not be hired. Then I make my recommendations, and to this day my clients have been invariably happy with them."

I trusted her intuitions, and got her to confirm my resume choices as well. When one of my hygienists moved to Vancouver, I needed to find a replacement. I advertised in the newspaper, and once again received many responses. The first candidate I met was very enthusiastic and I felt comfortable with her. Everything about her seemed to fit: her experience, the schedule, the pay. And so I hired her immediately. That same day, however, I went to meet my friend with the intuition and took the resumes I received along. She put her hand over them and presented me with her recommendation, saying, "This is number one, this is number two, and this one's going to give you trouble."

"Trouble," as it happened, was the woman I had hired! I went back to the office and told Daniela that we should meet with the other two applicants, in line with my friend's recommendations.

The next day I met with each of the other two candidates, and it turned out that the number one choice indicated by my friend, Nancy, couldn't work on the days we needed. I showed Nancy around the office anyway, and we talked at length. When she got home that evening, she looked at my web site and became very enthusiastic about the information on Reiki. She sent me an email the next morning saying, "I'd love to work with you, I'm going to change my working days if you are still willing to consider me." At the same time, the person I'd initially hired called and said that on second thought, she could not work with me because the times did not fit her schedule. She backed out and the way was cleared for my number one candidate. It all worked out effortlessly!

Nancy has since become a very popular staff member. Patients often call me to reveal how impressed they are with her skills and personality. Furthermore, since joining my staff, Nancy has taken it upon herself to study Reiki and other alternative therapies. Becoming a part of the office team has become a turning point in her life, and so not only has the practice gained an excellent team member, Nancy herself has found a new career direction that excites her.

My office has evolved substantially over the years, and from a one-woman show, my business has expanded to include seven other dentists, and altogether thirteen employees. I enjoy creating work for my team members, as well as to others who may provide various services. When a person approaches me regarding employment, I do my best to provide them with work. I believe it is important to help others in this sense as it creates business for them, and is likely to somehow provide business for me in turn, as an example of "giver's gain."

My team today is characterized by great diversity. We often joke amongst ourselves that we can almost form a new United Nations. As we all come from different regions and backgrounds, we speak eighteen languages between us, including sign language! It is truly remarkable how well we blend together, each contributing from their home culture, customs and religions. I believe my office is living proof that an efficient staff does not have to be comprised of people who are just like yourself. On the contrary, immeasurable benefits may be derived from diversity!

Chapter 8
Small Changes—Big Results

*"Do what you have always done and you'll get what
you have always gotten!"*
Sue Knight

You probably take the same route to your office every morning, simply out of habit. You have probably even stopped noticing things around you on this path, as you are already accustomed to the scenery. However, if one day, for whatever reason, you decide to travel by a different route you might encounter or notice something different which will present you with a new idea. This may be a building under construction or a sign with new information. Whatever it is, you've made a small change and have gained a new insight, which may seem inconsequential, but imagine how a multitude of minor changes could add up!

My office is on the fifth floor of a building with two elevators. Occasionally, one of them will be out of service, which often builds up a longer than usual wait. I therefore have gotten accustomed to taking the stairs up to my suite instead. This frequently saves me time and aggravation, not to mention that the extra exercise is good for my health.

When I walk through the elevator lobby and see a crowd waiting, I will jokingly say, "Hi guys, there is another option, a healthier one. I'm going up the stairs and you are welcome to join me." More often than not I get somewhat bewildered stares, though I haven't yet had anybody follow me into the stairwell! The other day, however, I went into the stairway and in followed a secretary from one of the other offices, one who I know to be a little shy. "You know," she said "I'm only doing this because of you. Since you suggested it, I've started going up the stairs every morning!"

I had inspired that person to make a change. It may have been small, but it made a difference for her all the same. This difference may have been the basis for other changes: perhaps her fitness level will improve, which may enhance her self-esteem, and on and on.

Another aspect which has transformed as a result of our meeting is our relationship. Instead of two strangers working in the same building, we now greet each other as friends whenever we happen to meet.

I have often noticed how small differences have had great influences in my patients' lives (besides the obvious comfort following a tooth ache treatment, of course). A patient whom I have not seen for several months will drop by and say, "You have made such a difference for me last time I was here. What you said changed my life!" There are times when I would ask the patient to recap our conversation from their previous visit, as these conversations, as significant as they turn out to be, are usually trivial dialogues. I must have said simply what came to my mind at the moment, which later turned out to be the right thing to say. I would sometimes find myself about to say something, and then think *Why should I say that?* We must remember, however, that we *are* each others' messengers and the most trivial piece of information you possess may turn out to be very consequential to another person. This is a two-way street, and I find that when I keep an open mind and listen, I can get good advice from others, who may be simply sharing their opinions or knowledge.

Over time, I learned that these conversations and exchanges of views and advice with patients could contribute greatly to their lives, adding value to their visit beyond the dental treatment. This can later contribute to my business as well, as not only has the relationship between the patient and I deepened with the communication and trust, but the patient may also be inclined to recommend me to others because of the advice I have given. I have since made it an integral part of my work to listen and try offering advice to my patients. They may either take it or leave it, but I find that it has strengthened the bond I share with my patients, enhancing their loyalty.

Although as people we are habitual creatures with the tendency to follow routines and habits, it is important to remember to constantly make small changes—for yourself and for others. These minor changes provide you with a different point of view and generate new ideas. These new ideas are the sources of more momentous changes that may lead to the transformation of your business and your life.

Chapter 9

The Team —
None of Us Is as Smart as All of Us

"Snowflakes are one of nature's most fragile things, but just look at what they can do when they stick together."
Vesta Kelly

Successful people always keep a team of advisors surrounding them. The President of the United States never makes a decision without advice. However, the President's advisors tend to be handpicked from elected officials or political party favorites. You get to choose yours from a much larger pool!

As I have mentioned earlier, we all have agents around us and generally in the "universe." It is only a matter of tapping into the advice they offer us. There are endless ways of achieving this, and here's an example that I have used and has proved to be very valuable.

About a year ago I organized a small group of people for meditation. Although each member had his or her individual goals, as we meditated together the group energy combined and we have all become stronger as a result. The outcome was so positive that we have since become a regular group of seven to ten people meeting every week for over a year now. Progressively, we became the advisory team for one another.

Aside from the power we derive from the meditation itself, we are constantly networking. People live their lives as part of many different groups, each consisting of different characters with an assortment of qualities. Each person in our group therefore, knows other people in other groups, who know others, and so on. The magic of this networking is that when you put out a need in one group, at least one of the people there is bound to know a person who may help.

For example, when I first came across the idea to write this book, I mentioned it during one of our meditating sessions. One friend who is part of the meditation group has introduced me to a publisher. Through another group, I met a person who specializes in marketing. And through yet another group, I met a writer.

Gradually I found that if you simply ask the people around you the right questions, you will get the right connections for your purposes, enabling you to realize your goals.

These people, all around you, are your advisory team. One person will have many different teams, composed of friends, family, colleagues and so forth. Each of these people has their own team of spiritual advisors, which they bring into play when they join up with an earthly team. By combining forces with your earthly team members, and including each person's spiritual advisors, a staggering power is created!

I have always believed that it is imperative that you surround yourself with the finest people. That is why I am so satisfied and proud of my office staff. Building a team you can trust and rely on multiplies the possibilities that are out there for you exponentially.

A friend of mine from the Women Entrepreneurs Association has a very different background than I do and possesses a whole set of diverse talents. One day, the Canadian Women Entrepreneurs received an invitation to attend a public hearing in Canada's House of Commons regarding bank mergers. As I was Vice President of the organization, I was asked by my friend to assist in making a response. At first I felt a little jammed, since as a dentist, what on earth did I know about bank mergers? However, I *did* know that my friend is knowledgeable in this field, and with her help we quickly got a team together, compiled statistics, and performed interviews. In a very short time the team built a complete presentation.

My friend has become a source of stimulation and knowledge for me, and over the years I have learned a lot from her. I must admit, however, that when we first met, I found her eloquence and skills rather intimidating. Now that I have learned to recognize different talents in other people, I have come to realize that different people have various skills that can complement my own skills. Following the House of Commons hearing, this friend confided in me and said that she could not have attended the hearing without me continuously and fearlessly telling her, "Let's do it!" On the other hand, I would not have been able to attend the hearing on my own, since while I may be "fearless," I do not know the first thing about bank mergers, let alone addressing the issue to members of Parliament. By tackling the challenge as a team, I supplied the emotional support for her, and she eloquently made the presentation. Although we are completely different people, the joining of my friend and I in this project created a combined energy that we applied to achieve our mutual goals.

I am positive that each of you has experienced a similar situation at some point, in which you have noticed that your energy rises when you are around a certain person. This person may be your spouse, a friend, or a co-worker, and when you are together, everything seems to flow and positive things tend to occur. These are the kind of people you want to recruit to your team.

You may be wondering, *How do I recognize potential members for my team?* Although different people may use different methods of selection, I find that for me, it is a matter of intuition — when I meet someone, I just know in my gut whether or not they may be of help to me or the other way around — me being of help to them. I trust my instincts and I am confident that when I need help, an opportunity will present itself.

A few years ago, I bought a condo to rent out as an investment. I aimed to get the place in shape to rent out in time for the film festival that was about to take place in the area. This was rather ambitious as I only had ten days. As it happened, a new patient mentioned that she was looking for work as an interior designer. Right away, I said, "Let me finish your X-rays and examination, and I have a job for you."

Immediately following her appointment, we went to look at the apartment. My new interior designer connected me immediately with carpenters, painters and carpet layers, and the renovation and redecoration of the place was all done in time for the film festival. Furthermore, when I called the rental office I was allocated a tenant instantaneously.

Another example of a staff member who complements me, and is, quite frankly indispensable, is my office manager Daniela. Everybody has faults, and one of mine is that I was never very careful with money. I have a tendency to be somewhat of a spendthrift at times. Since I do not pay attention to little things, I could not state the price of a quart of milk or anything, for that matter.

I realize the importance of remembering numbers and dates and would love to possess that ability, but over the years I have come to terms with the fact that I am just not built that way. I make decisions solely based on gut feelings. Luckily, one of these gut feelings was to hire Daniela, who is very price conscious and knowledgeable regarding the many methods of saving money on purchases. That is the reason we are different and also why she complements me so wholly.

While I may be seen as the dreamer or visionary, Daniela has been blessed with grounded, realistic common sense. We respect each other's distinctions and feel that we balance each other with our diverse skills. Although people may have a tendency to seek others who will agree with them on every aspect, the people who benefit you most and contribute to your growth are the ones who say "no" and think differently than you. By surrounding yourself with diverse people, you expose yourself to new points of view and learn to see things with new perspectives.

The level of trust and confidence between Daniela and I has allowed for near telepathic synchronisctic events to take place between the two of us, as we are both aware of the other's needs and expectations. The other day, for example, I had to go to a Women Entrepreneurs meeting, so I left my office early and went home to get my car, as I live only two minutes away from my office. I got in my car, but instead of taking the shortest route as I usually do, I mistakenly went one extra block before turning south. As a result, I was sitting in traffic at a stoplight near my office when I looked out and saw Daniela crossing the street and walking toward me smiling. As it turns out, she had been trying to call me, but my cell phone was turned off. She needed me to sign the new assistant's paycheck. It was the assistant's first pay, and as she was new in the country she needed the check urgently. When Daniela stepped up to the window, she said, "I've been trying to reach you. Do you have a check for the new assistant?" Right there in the traffic light, I found and signed the check on the steering wheel and handed it to her. Then the light turned green and I continued on my way downtown.

The whole issue could not have worked out better if we'd planned it! Daniela had a need and put it out there. That request was immediately manifested when she found me at a place where I would not normally have been. Amazing? Perhaps. But then, Daniela and I are on each other's team!

Another team I belong to which has contributed greatly to my business and personal life is *Business Networking International* (BNI). BNI has local chapters worldwide, which meet weekly with the purpose of making business referrals between the members of the chapter. Needless to say, I learned a lot about networking and I got a lot of new patients through the referrals. What's more, I also met people whose services I could use, people who have helped me build my business and who I can recommend to others. I keep a whole rack of business cards of the people I recommend in my waiting room. These are not necessarily just health and wellness practitioners, the cards cover all types of services. I have such an established network of people to recommend that when I get to know a patient's needs, I actively go and pick out the cards to give to them.

I had a patient this week that wanted to come for a long time but hadn't been able to. I had been treating her extensively, but she had become extremely busy and missed some appointments. When she finally came in, her gums looked quite bad, partly because of the stress she was under. She realized what was happening, but people sometimes don't react to things as they should. If their routine gets disrupted, they stop exercising and making time for themselves. Your body can create problems when it is out of balance. The problems differ by individual but usually involve the weakest area. Some people start grinding their teeth and get pains in the neck. At the same time, the thing that caused the stress, and that subsequently caused the dental problem, requires attention. These people may have a need or a problem that's stressing them and they can use some advice. If I can help by giving my advice or a referral, I am happy to do so.

This particular lady wanted to start a business. She was employed and had no time to pursue her goal, and she had stopped doing the things she should have been doing for her own peace of mind. We started talking and I advised her to take care of her own needs first. She realized that she needed to get back to exercising and meditating daily right away. She needed to create a balance and make time for herself.

Next we got to talking about her business. "I have people I know who you should meet." I said, and gave her some business cards. She needed financing, so I gave her a financing contact. She needed an accountant, and I was able to recommend one. I told her to mention my name, as all these people know me. That was a good start for her and I was glad to be able to help.

I guess you could call this the practice of truly holistic dentistry. Holistic means everything connected — your gums are connected to your immune system, which is connected to your stress level, which is influenced by your lifestyle at the moment.

At this stage, I have a business that is growing. Instead of one dentist and an assistant, we are now seven associates, two hygienists and four other employees. Moreover, there are several contract employees: a web site designer, an interior decorator, a Feng Shui expert, a handyman, a marketing person and so on. As my team has expanded over the years, my position within it has shifted, demanding me to exercise different leadership and managerial skills which I may not have needed to master before.

Some may argue that leadership and managerial skills are innate. I believe that with learning and experience, most people can step up to the challenge and succeed. Although some will put their faith into business schools, for example, to teach them various management skills, I found that for me the most effective method was by experimentation and experience. The Women Entrepreneurs of Canada (WEC) provided me with this opportunity, teaching me about finances, organizational politics, employment laws, policies, ethics, effective decision making, and becoming a leader. During the five years I have been a member of the WEC, I have become a Board Member, an International Representative, Vice President, and finally President of the organization.

Aside from my dental clinic, I have begun experimenting in other businesses, such as purchasing condominiums for rent. I do not know a lot about the apartment rental business, however, I do have a team consisting of an agent, lawyer and accountant, all of whom provide me with any information I may need to make an educated decision. My responsibility in this case is to provide my team with a general direction of where I would like to be or accomplish, and give the final word in major decisions, inline with their recommendations, since without them I could be lost — that is why it is vital to listen and learn from the different teams you have working around you.

An effective and powerful team is a team which is well-connected, meaning all members put forth whatever it is they are looking for from the team and can offer to the team. The concept of "giver's gain" comes into play here — when you give or offer anything to your team members, the probability that you will get something in return will grow exponentially. If you will look after your team members, they are likely to look after you and your needs.

Chapter 10
Making Choices — Trusting Your Instincts

"It is through science that we prove,
but through intuition that we discover."
Henri Poincare

Every one of us is faced with decisions that can alter our careers and life every day. Some of these decisions may seem trivial while others may prove to be difficult and complex. People have different ways and methods of making decisions: some may resort to making pros and cons lists while others will determine their fate at the flip of a coin. As I mentioned earlier, I find that the most effective method for me is gathering any relevant information and then simply trusting my gut instincts, confident that my team of advisors will come through with the right guidance.

I was not always so secure and self-assured of my instincts, however. Trusting that everything will work out some way or other requires taking a leap of faith, which took me a long time to dare take. Once I became gradually more comfortable in trusting my instincts, I realized how many aspects of my life, and particularly decision making, have become much easier. One aspect, which made a significant difference for me, was delegating. When you personally select the people on your team, you can easily trust in them making delegation responsibilities easier, which in turn takes the load off your back and improves the flow and efficiency of your business.

Just as in any other aspect of life, practice makes perfect. While trusting your instincts will never be an exact science, I believe you can train yourself to become more aware of the direction your instincts are pointing at and learn to become increasingly confident in your instinctual abilities. I have developed a small game, or exercise, which I use to prove to myself continuously the power and accuracy of my gut feelings. I do this using my set of keys, which comprises six identical keys for different purposes. Of course, the easy solution would have been to mark the keys with color-coded tags, for example, but that would be too easy! Instead, I trust my instincts to help me choose the right key every time. Whenever I need to open a door, I grab the key I feel will work and surprisingly, nine times out of ten, I will choose the right one! Since I am confident in my instincts to choose the right key, I seldom fail. That said, however, I do notice that at times when I am stressed or anxious, I seldom choose the right key.

We have all heard about the benefits of positive thinking. While some people may refer to it as "luck," all it really is, is maintaining a positive attitude. A person who concentrates on positive things will attract good things. A person who focuses on negative things, however, will tend to encounter them. Positive thinking is the power of attraction, of sending off good vibrations, and this is the key to making wise choices.

When I was faced with the decision of whether or not to ask my husband for a divorce, it was a painful deliberation. I struggled to remain as positive as possible and looked forward to the positive outcomes. Divorce is generally seen as a negative process, but I decided to approach it as the chance to make positive changes in my life—to be happier, grow personally, and pursue my career. Although the process was painful for the whole family, it was a learning opportunity, and now, years later, my ex-husband and my daughters all agree that it worked out for the best.

The decision to file for divorce proved to be such a difficult one since I was not the only one affected by it, but rather my whole family, including my daughters, one of whom was still very young. I had to trust that not only was I making the right decision for myself, but for the rest of my family as well. This decision is of course a lot more monumental than simply choosing the right key for a door, but I had to trust my gut feeling in this much larger issue. I had faith that my guides in the universe were sending me clues to look for—small hints that would help with making the decision, providing some guidance and direction.

During the stressful period of the divorce, for example, I sometimes found encouragement and comfort in dreams. The day before I was due in court to finalize my divorce, I dreamed of a baby crying in the basement. I felt that the baby had been crying for a long time, so I went downstairs and held it, feeling a massive amount of love. I felt that this was a positive sign. The crying baby was the child in me that I had ignored. I had been ignoring my own feelings and needs. I felt that by finalizing the divorce, I would become free to concentrate on my needs and ambitions.

I realized then that I was making the right decision about the divorce. The dream took away any feelings of doubt and switched my whole being to positive. The divorce was something that was good for me, and was long overdue. When you make certain decisions, it is good if they come from self-love. Those decisions are truly the best!

These clues have also been there to support and guide my decision to purchase my first investment condo. One day, while I was in the process of selling my house, a patient told me about a small condominium she knew was up for sale in her building. In her opinion, the price quoted was lower than the market value, but since the unit had been offered for sale for a long time, the owners had just lowered the price again. Following the appointment, she took me to see the apartment, which surprisingly turned out to the apartment right across the hall from my ex-husband's!

I considered what a coincidence it was that of all the condominiums for sale in such a large city I was referred to this one, and decided to treat the coincidence as a clue, a sign for me to pay attention that there might be more to this deal than I first imagined. Today, after acquiring that condominium and several other investment condos following, I appreciate the signs that were given me which directed me towards the acquisition, as the investment had turned out to be fruitful, and has introduced me to whole new business opportunities in real estate.

Trusting your instincts and spotting the clues can work for any sort of decision, from insignificant choices to major life altering decisions. For example, I have met with a person whom I was considering for appointment to a committee I was on, and I was contemplating whether that person would make a worthy addition to the group. While reflecting on this decision, I happened to glance at a newspaper nearby, and on the front page I spotted the last name of that person. I accepted that as a sign and confirmation regarding the choice I was making. As it turned out, this person has later proved to be a very vital person to the organization.

At another time, I hired a contractor to lay a new floor in one of my condos days before I was supposed to travel to Europe. I was debating whether to wait with the renovation project until my return, as I was supposed to be gone for over a month, and I felt slightly uncomfortable about leaving the team of renovators unsupervised. As I was contemplating my decision while driving home one night, I spotted the unusual name of the contractor on the license plate of a passing car. I considered this a confirmation to my decision, and needless to say, everything worked out smoothly.

To assist us in our decisions, the universe and our agents supply us with the clues that are rarely simple answers, but rather sorts of helpers or guides. People search for these signs in different ways, some using Tarot cards, astrology, or others who may plainly open a book and spot a random word on the page to which they can provide meaning that further guides them in their decision. The more you learn to trust your instincts, the less you need to search for and rely on the helpers. Like any other skill, it is merely a matter of practice to gain the insight.

Choices and decision-making are also closely connected to timing, which is in turn closely related to intuition. In other words, a decision you may take at a specific moment may not be so fruitful or suitable for other times. For example, when I first purchased my practice in Toronto, my financial situation was so strained that upgrading equipment was completely out of the question. As I understood this, I did not consciously think about the different facilities and equipment that may need upgrading. One day, however, while I was treating a patient, I pulled on a suction tube that was stuck. The patient commented on my old equipment and I realized that by not upgrading my tools I was not making a good impression. While I wanted to convey to my patients that the office is keeping up with the latest technology and innovations in the field, my equipment was sending a different and conflicting message. By that time my income had been increasing steadily, and upgrading was now feasible. I was now able to make the decision to upgrade, which may not have been the right decision earlier, but had definite positive results at present.

Another example of how timing is crucial in decision-making is regarding future planning. A couple of years after I had opened my dental clinic in Toronto, I began putting some thought and resources into planning the future direction and activity of the office. At that time my clinic operated three dental chairs, and according to the yearly growth of patients coming to the office, I predicted that the three operatories would become insufficient in the near future. The clinic needed to expand in order to accommodate future business effectively. Luckily, as soon as I had come to this realization, I learned that the office next to mine would be soon vacated, providing me with the ideal opportunity for expansion.

A few years ago a woman was referred to me by one of my friends. The new patient was in terrible pain and had been to two other clinics prior to seeing me. One of these clinics has simply provided the patient with antibiotics before sending her away, while the other would not treat her without advance payment.

When this woman first walked into my office she stated that she could not afford to pay for the treatment in advance, although she could make installments for a period of time. In my examination I noticed immediately that she required a root canal critically. "You're in terrible pain," I said, "Let's help you to get rid of the pain and worry about the payments later." Although I have never met this woman before, something about her gave me a positive feeling that I could trust her. As it turned out, my gut feeling regarding this woman was correct, as I completed her treatment and she duly paid all her installments. In time she began referring other patients, including her family and friends, proving that by extending her credit, which was a relatively small risk and awarded me initially with the satisfaction of helping someone, I gained many new patients, making the rewards much greater than anticipated.

My advice is to simply trust your instincts when making a decision. If you feel good with the decision you are making, it is probably the right one for you. As I mentioned earlier, though, instincts and gut feelings are not an exact science, and mistakes happen occasionally. Sometimes a decision you make may turn out to have negative implications, while other situations are known ahead of time to be "lose-lose" situations. However, any decision is good if you approach it in a positive light. After all, we make our own "luck"!

Chapter 11
Walking Your Path —
Your Own Balancing Act

*"Happiness in life is not measured by the things we achieved,
the places we go or the route that we take to get there.
Happiness in life is measured by the people
that we share all of our experiences with."*
Chris Needham

One of the many dangers business owners face is becoming completely immersed in work at the expense of everything else: family, friends and other interests. Being busy is addictive, and without noticing you may get sucked into continuously being occupied. As with any other addiction, being excessively absorbed in your business will make you feel guilty and can destroy your relationships.

There are a variety of ways to gain success in your business that are easier and healthier than working yourself to death. I believe in the method of exerting least effort by balancing the business and family life and by remembering to occasionally take the time away from the office to spend exclusively on the other aspects of your life: family, friends, hobbies, and so forth. By applying this strategy of work, you can, not only achieve your goals, but you will also maximize your gratification and fulfillment from the journey.

Learning to balance business and family is crucial, particularly for women today who wish to raise a family as well as pursue a successful career. I believe that although building a business is a challenging task for anyone, women are faced with even more difficulties, as traditionally they are more immersed in the day-to-day running and maintaining of the family home.

One of the ways I found which assisted in balancing my family life with the development of my practice was by integrating my daughters in the business. As I indicated earlier, each one of my daughters found her own "niche" in the office, one responsible for the bookkeeping and reception, another specialized in the technical aspects and the youngest one providing us with much entertainment and delight, making the whole experience enjoyable as well as productive.

Integrating my daughters in my business turned out to be a "win-win-win" situation. Not only did the girls assist me greatly in developing the office, maintaining an efficient flow of things and raising my productivity and profits, but it allowed me to balance the time spent in the office and the time spent with my family. Lastly, and perhaps most importantly, it provided my daughters with a considerable learning experience of the entrepreneurial world as well as inspiration. By watching me build my business from scratch, and by understanding the methods and tools I used for this, they became motivated that if they only put their mind to it, they will be able to succeed as well.

My daughters each have a very unique character and each one of them is attracted to other fields and possess a variety of different talents. The two elder daughters, Shirrah and Kinneret, are currently pursuing their bachelor degrees in universities in Canada and Holland. They have taken the experience and knowledge they have acquired in my office into their ventures in school and work. The younger daughter, Tamar, is currently excelling in high school, and since she is the only one left at home, I can see how my experiences with my business have affected and developed her own entrepreneurial skills.

When she was about nine years old, Tamar would often suffer headaches, stomach aches, and so on. Whenever she would feel ill, she would tag along with me to work. I would bring pillows and blankets and set them up in my private office to let her sleep. One day, during one of her sick days in the office, Tamar suddenly remembered a school assignment that needed to be done regarding fundraising. Right there in the office she prepared a flyer and began canvassing people as they came off the elevator.

Later that year I found Tamar in her room counting a large amount of money. When I inquired about it, I learned of the Heart and Stroke Foundation fundraising competition. It turned out that Tamar and a friend had been jumping rope in front of a café in a shopping plaza in order to raise money from passersby. Although every person contributed a very small amount, they had managed to raise nearly one hundred and fifty dollars! At that moment I understood how much she has learned from me simply from coming with me to the office. Tamar may have been too young to understand the ropes of the business and was usually only an onlooker in the office, but she did learn that by manifesting your goals you can gradually achieve them, and she applied this life lesson in her assignments for school, with much success.

You cannot teach someone to be somebody that they are not, but you can show them the way. It was beneficial for my kids to see and experience how I work. Not only did this provide them with useful work experience and the motivation and confidence that they can be successful in anything they decide to do, but it made things easier for myself as well. By integrating them, my family understands my business and appreciates what I do. I get the pleasure and benefits of having my daughters near me, and they gain insight and useful knowledge that will assist them in their future endeavors.

Integrating your family and business is not enough, though. You must ensure to occasionally take time off from work to spend exclusively with your family. Even during times when you think you cannot afford the time away from the business, you *must* take it, since once it passes, you will never get it back. Once again, letting go of the business and spending time with your family requires trusting that everything will work out for the best by taking the time off, even if it may not seem this way.

Some people state that life is hard and you have to earn your bread with the sweat of your brow. I believe that by saying this, these people are manifesting that situation. If you believe you have to work hard, then you will have to. On the other hand, if you apply a method of less effort by concentrating on your goal but spending time and energy on the other aspects of your life such as family, friends, sports and so forth, this way of life will become a part of you. You will cultivate a mental state of relaxation, which will make the journey towards achieving your goals a great deal easier and more enjoyable.

Chapter 12
Positive Vibrations —
The Thing Called "Luck"

"I've found that luck is quite predictable."
Brian Tracy

The word "luck" is often used to describe circumstances of something positive happening in a sudden way. Although there are people whom others refer to as "lucky," I believe that no one is born naturally lucky or unlucky, but rather we make our own luck by sending out vibrations and by that influencing our fortune.

The vibrations and ambiance you spread create the atmosphere surrounding you. This explains why some people are easier to be around with than others. The way you think determines the vibrations you emit as well as the outcomes you attract. By concentrating on positive things, you are likely to attract good things. If you are constantly worried, you generate obstructions that will prevent you from reaching your goals as well as avert positive thinking in the future. It is a vicious circle!

Thinking positive is no easy task. It requires persistence and at times proves to be very difficult to achieve. To remain continually positive you have to be able to see things from a different angle. Some events may seem negative at first, but in reality develop into blessings in disguise! Even if this is not the case, you should learn to regard any situation as a learning experience. Once you learn to appreciate the challenges, you can turn any challenge or hardship into an opportunity! When I first opened my practice in Toronto, for example, I could have sat in my office, dwelling on my lack of patients accompanied by high overhead and loans. Nobody can tell how the future would have turned out in that scenario, however, my guess is that it would not have led me to my position today as effectively.

People who consider themselves unlucky, therefore, should not sit around feeling sorry for themselves, nor wait for the winds to change. All they need to do is change their mindset from dwelling on what is lacking in their lives, to reflecting upon what is abundant in their lives. Once they begin to comprehend how much is positive in their lives, they will begin to send off positive vibes.

Astrology also deals with the concept of luck, claiming that luck may come easily at some times and periods rather than others, depending on the person's time and place of birth, the alignment of the planets both at the time of birth and currently. I benefit greatly from consulting an astrologer occasionally as the map she draws up for me indicates which times are considered "luckier" for me. In this way, if I have a large project due or major decision to make, I try to aim for one of the lucky times.

The other day I went to the hairdresser. The man who does my hair is the owner of the salon, and he seemed to be having a rough day, annoyed with one of the employees. I do not know whether this man is interested in spirituality, but that day he said to me, "You know, this business keeps me stressed all the time, but when I'm working on your hair, I feel relaxed."

Although it would be great, I realize my hair does not possess any special healing powers! However, there was something about my energy that relaxed him. I believe that this calm, peaceful aura is what my patients often feel, as they are often very close to me during treatment. The energy I send off is sometimes so tranquil that I've had patients fall asleep in the dental chair. I once had three patients in a row that fell asleep — the middle one had come in for a twenty-minute appointment!

Each person's aura is different. While it is beneficial to maintain a positive energy, it is also valuable to emit an aura that promotes trust. By transmitting that you are trustworthy, you will attract similar people — people who will trust you and whom you can trust in return. By cultivating relationships with others with mutual trust, nearly everything about running the business will become easier: delegating responsibilities to employees, making business deals, and so forth.

I believe in the saying "What goes around comes around." We should all do our best to transmit our positive thoughts and energy, cleanse our aura, that some people refer to as Karma. Eliminate the negative, mistrusts and self-serving agendas. Keep in mind your personal integrity, honesty and ethics, and I guarantee you will seize the key to long-term success in any aspect of your life, your emotions, general well-being, and the harmony you create for yourself and for others.

Chapter 13
Moving Forward — Conquering Your Fears

"He who fears he will suffer, already suffers from his fear."
Michel de Montaigne

Everyone has fears. When I was younger I had a fear of heights. Whenever I had to cross a bridge and could see the bottom through the cracks, I would get so frightened that the only way I could cross was by crawling. Later in my life, I decided to take up skiing, and despite my fear of heights I went skiing in the Alps. Going up the lift terrified me, and skiing down even more, but eventually I managed to do it. I forced myself to overcome my fear, slowly gaining confidence. Today, as a result, I am no longer afraid of heights (or at least not as much).

The same applies to fear of public speaking. When I was younger, I was petrified of talking to even a group of three people whom I did not know. It was nearly impossible for me to open my mouth and formulate sentences. It is hard to believe that nowadays I speak in public often, and am not that bad at it either!

It is interesting to see how things can change when you put your mind to it. Another phenomenon I have observed is the inclination of some people to be most attracted to the things they fear the most. I believe that this attraction is our natural desire to overcome these fears, instead of hiding from them. My recipe for overcoming our fears is simple: deal with them. Most likely you will come to the realization that there was nothing to be afraid of in the first place. Fear will always crop up, but do not let it hold you back—work through it.

All the things you find negative in life or in business are based on a fear: a fear of trusting people or situations, or losing what you have: money, possessions, reputation, and the list goes on and on.

The first step in disposing of your fears is to create a state of mind where your first priority is not to accumulate things. This applies to anything in life: clothing, objects, bad habits and fears. Rather than holding onto things, get into the practice of circulating what you have and what you are. When you circulate and give things up, good things come back many fold. That is a promise.

If you are afraid of trusting the world, transform your fear into positive thinking and emit positive vibes. Once you change your energy field, your thinking, attitudes and behavior patterns are likely to be next. Once you shed off all your shells, covers and walls, you affect your environment by attracting people who are like you. In the business world, you will attract business partners and employees that are like you. They may have different skills, of course, but you can trust that they will do their best to serve the organization or the company, just like you.

As an entrepreneur, you must always be fearless. *Easier said than done*, you must be thinking. But if you are not, act as though you are. Eventually it will become your second nature. Over time you will reach a stage where you are less afraid of making mistakes. This does not mean that you will not make some mistakes along the way — you can be sure that you will. The key is not to fear them. Successful people learn from their mistakes and take defeat as a challenge and an opportunity.

When you deal with people, you may occasionally say the wrong thing — there is always someone who may be offended. Some people are just built this way. They have become accustomed to believing they are victims, and offending them is therefore bound to happen. If this happens, take the high road and profess that your sincere intention was not to offend them. It is important to rectify the situation without delay. This applies to all situations in life — you need to have the courage to amend any situation immediately, no matter how awkward, painful or embarrassing. If you feel something has gone wrong in a relationship or in business, do not put it away and wait for it to resolve on it's own. Ask what is wrong. Keep things out in the open, and do not let your fear of dealing with the problem prevent you from dealing with it.

I have learned a great deal about handling such problems from my friend. While we were at an international conference connected with the Women Entrepreneurs of Canada, there were representatives from some thirty different countries. My friend was reporting on the situation in her country, when the woman representing an African country became offended about the subject of membership fees. She stood up and irately stated how difficult it was for her to transfer money from her country. She felt that we were not aware of the difficulties some people have. My friend recovered the situation very quickly by saying, "I sincerely had no intention to offend anyone. As you may know, I was born in the Far East, and I have encountered the same complexities you are describing now." The woman was pacified, feeling that she was understood and that others were sympathetic to her situation. Following the meeting, several people offered her help with the problem.

I was immeasurably impressed with the way my friend handled the delicate situation. She had taken control and turned what could have been a problematical and disruptive situation into a calm one, in which a solution could be sought. I admired her fearlessness. Later that evening we had a chance to talk some more. She told me many things I was not aware of regarding business: how to create a public company, financial terms and other concepts. I was deeply impressed with her knowledge and told her so. That was when she said something that had completely caught me by surprise—she claimed to have learned to be fearless from me! I had never thought of myself as fearless before, especially given my history with heights and public speaking. But my friend insisted that although she observed that I sometimes seemed to be afraid, I had always gone forward. That is what I am recommending here.

Some people need extra help in overcoming fears. Fear of the dentist is one that I encounter every day! I found a way around that by practicing Reiki on my patients to calm them. I once treated an eleven-year-old girl who had been in a car accident and was severely traumatized by it. She had gone through many painful medical treatments and among other things, had broken her front tooth and needed a root canal. Her parents brought her in to see me, but I could not do anything as she was completely paralyzed by fear. I decided to practice Reiki on her to help her relax.

To those of you who are not familiar with the practice, Reiki is a method of using your hands to channel energy from the universe. It is not my energy, but a universal energy which balances and heals. After having done the Reiki the girl was relaxed, and I was able to finish the treatment. In this case, I had alleviated the little girl's fear by using Reiki, which allowed her to receive the treatment she needed.

You can allow yourself to overcome your fears by recognizing them and facing up to them. Remember that your fears hold you back from taking the steps than will lead you to success. Channel your positive energy into overcoming your fears and move forward. The benefits are enormous. You will not regret it.

Chapter 14
Branding — Leaving Your Mark on It

"A product is something made in a factory; a brand is something that is bought by the consumer. A product can be copied by a competitor; a brand is unique. A product can be quickly outdated; a successful brand is timeless."
Stephen King

As a dentist I am regarded as an authority figure. That is why when I first started practicing Reiki, I perceivably had much more credibility than perhaps some others would, and I felt privileged that I could open up other's lives to spirituality.

As I practiced Reiki, many things began to evolve around me. At first I began doing it for pleasure as a new relaxation technique, until a patient told me that while I was practicing it on him he felt a huge surge of vigor, as if he was floating. This patient confided in me that for several months he was feeling very stressed due to some personal problems. He has been to several doctors after a long period of weariness, but now, after the Reiki, he suddenly felt refreshed and energized.

I remember thinking at the time, *Wow! I never imagined Reiki could have such a powerful effect!*

Another time I was working on another patient, and I happened to be thinking of something funny while I was doing Reiki on her and waiting for the anesthetic to take effect. The patient, who had been nervous about having dental work done said, "It's very odd. I've been in a bad mood all day but now I feel like dancing!"

During that period I was gradually becoming aware of how my mood and state of mind was being conveyed to my patients through Reiki. After some time I had a realization. I thought, *Here is the perfect tool to use in my dental practice, a niche that will make me unique, differentiate me from the other dentists, and bring business my way.* That is how I created my business "brand" using the energy of Reiki to deal in a natural, holistic way with patients' fear. Once people who had previously been afraid of going to the dentist experienced the calming effect of Reiki, they informed others who were similarly afraid, and my list of patients expanded.

Although I did not plan it initially, it turned out that my decision to become a Reiki master became the answer as to how to make my business successful. Once again, the universe had been helping me in an inventive way.

I practice Reiki not only on my patients, but also on the patients of other practitioners working in my building who perform extractions or surgeries. Their patients often come see me before their appointments simply to relax. In general, Reiki does more than getting them through their appointments, it promotes healing. The stress of surgery or an extraction is detrimental to healing. It deprives your body of the energy needed to heal itself. Reiki can make the difference.

Reiki became my brand completely by chance. Although I grasped the concept of Reiki early on, it took me a while before I realized the potential and opportunity it provided me for developing my business. Today my dental clinic is known for its practice of Reiki for calming nervous patients. The branding and differentiation of the clinic as such has earned me many patients over the years. I should add that all of my staff and associates have since studied Reiki voluntarily. They too find it very beneficial in their work and the satisfaction of the patients has been significantly enhanced.

Another thing that seems to please my patients is the range of photos I have on the walls. As I have participated in many courses with Deepak Chopra, Wayne Dyer and others, I like to display the photos taken at the Pyramids in Egypt, Ghoa in India and other exotic sites. The pictures often spur conversation and frequently lead to interesting exchanges. These discussions often provide me with a chance to offer advice or recommend places where patients may seek further assistance on some matter.

A third part of my branding strategy includes the rack of business cards I keep in the reception area. I wish my patients to view my office as an "oasis" of tranquility, a caring atmosphere where they can receive top-notch dental care as well as obtain help and advice on other day-to-day problems. This is my brand, and it distinguishes my office and me from all other dentists.

Just as I noticed the effect that Reiki had on my patients and comprehended the great potential it had for my business, it is important that you continually experiment with new things, recognizing and grabbing the opportunities that come your way. Don't just sit there and wonder when the right opportunity will come. Always be on the lookout. Seek it actively. And eventually, when you will recognize it don't hesitate to grab it.

Chapter 15

In Conclusion —
The Final and Ultimate Ingredient for Success

"There are some people who live in a dream world,
and there are some who face reality;
and then there are those who turn one into the other."
Douglas Everett

If you have read this far, you must know a great deal about some of the things I believe in, and which have molded me into the person I am today. I have written about manifesting success, recruiting staff, financing, and many other things that have helped me create and develop my practice. There is one more element, however, that is vital to your success. This is perhaps the most important ingredient of all—you.

We all arrive in the world with a pre-determined plan of which we are not aware. In other words, everyone has a purpose in life that they must fulfill in order to keep things in balance. The tricky part is that since we arrive at the outset with no knowledge of what it is we have to do—we must somehow figure it out for ourselves along the way.

When I was a child in Finland, I had a consuming interest in herbs and plants that could be used for healing. I had no idea where this interest came from, nor did my parents. I loved strolling through the woods near my home searching for plants that I could make remedies of (more or less). I knew the names of hundreds of them by heart and wished to know the uses for each one. I felt safest and happiest wandering among those trees and plants—I still do. The forest is a renewing and healing place for me. Is it any wonder that I went into healthcare?

In retrospect, the signs were all there. I had an overriding interest in plant life and my favorite teachers at school were the ones who taught botany and sciences. I merely had to pay attention to where my interests emerged from and follow my instincts. This was not as easy as it sounds, though. It took me many years before I understood entirely what my future direction would be— I would not have guessed for the life of me that it would be in dentistry!

Today I can appreciate what a suitable choice I have made. Dentistry allows me to be independent and entrepreneurial rather than work as a part of a larger group, as a doctor in a hospital, for example.

When I first chose a career in dentistry, I spent the first years learning the technical skills. Later, with the experience came the communication skills and after that the entrepreneurial and leadership skills. I love running a business and employing staff. More recently, I have felt a need to share my knowledge further by writing this book.

As a teenager, I thought I had been born in the wrong place. I had difficulty identifying with Finnish culture and traditions. I needed to see things from a different perspective and it was not until I had moved to Israel, and become more aware of things and others around me, that I began to fully understand myself. I began to appreciate that by being born in Finland, I was offered the opportunity to cultivate my interest in woodland plants and herbs, as Finland is rich in wooded areas I could explore. It was the right place for me to be born after all. And once I recognized my purpose in life, I have never looked back.

Everyone needs to find out their reason for being here, and get on with the task. You do not need to sit on a mountain in Katmandu to discover your purpose—the answer is in you. Being aware of the clues around you will assist you in that discovery. My clue was my interest in plants. Yours will be something completely different. The key is to simply pay attention. Ask yourself, *What are my interests? What intrigues me? What lifts my spirits?* The answers to these questions are the beginning to knowing yourself and discovering your purpose in life.

I have said before that in order to be successful, you must release the things that block you from moving ahead. Everyone has potential, but I estimate that the average person makes use of about ten percent of it. Understanding that there are spiritual guides in the universe, part of your team, who are there to help you, is not enough. You must ask for their help—they will not step in uninvited. The first step is therefore to clear hesitation and any other blocks that may keep you from communicating with your guides. Be positive. Have the faith and confidence that you know what is right. Do not be afraid of making a mistake once in a while—it is all a part of the learning process!

You need to make a daily commitment to yourself and the universe. Take some time every morning and think, *I commit to doing my best* or *I commit to being positive*. Put these thoughts out there. Some people would say this out loud while others would prefer to say it silently or write it down. Whichever way you choose, you must fully believe in it and truly make the commitment.

In time, the commitment and faith will become easier, until they become an integral part of you. Sincerity and persistence is the key. Do not practice this out of habit, simply going through the motions — this will never work, and may even backfire by leading to frustration and thus negative energy. Consciously maintain a healthy, positive attitude, and before long you will be emitting positive vibes that will invite good things to happen to you. Exercising you values, such as being genuine and truthful, make the vibrations more powerful and the manifesting even stronger.

I believe one of the reasons my patients enjoy coming to my office is the positive atmosphere. It is a cheerful place filled with pleasant, serene vibes. This should be true in any business. Make sure your office or clinic is a place in which people feel comfortable and wish to return and conduct business with you. Sure, the place must be clean, efficient, and nicely decorated, but that's not all—your staff and overall atmosphere must be pleasant and positive. To accomplish this you must treat your team well. Be sure they are fulfilled and satisfied in their work, and provide them with a pleasant environment to work in. Trust them. Empower them to make decisions. By proving your team with the power, opportunity and freedom to grow, they too will be giving off the positive vibes to which your clients will respond, enabling your business to become more successful.

Do not be afraid to ask your spiritual helpers for guidance, but be clear when you do. Explore the questions you wish to ask fully. Be sure you know what it is you seek to find out or what it is you wish to achieve. This way, you'll be sure to recognize the answers when they arrive.

Answers may come in a variety of forms. At one point I was offered a clue in a dream. I was concerned about how my relationship with Michael, the man in my life, was evolving. I was feeling anxious because things did not seem to be progressing as I had hoped they would. I put the question out to my spiritual advisors and soon after, I had a dream. Michael and I were swimming and the water was smooth and calm, but soon I noticed there were jagged rocks in the waters ahead. Michael was following me, but I realized that if I would keep swimming ahead we would be in trouble. I suddenly noticed Michael motioning for me to follow him and I changed course. Soon the water became calm again and the jagged rocks disappeared. We were safe. I reflected on that dream the next day and the answer was clear. I had been too determined to have things go my way. I needed to take Michael's lead occasionally and let him do more, be less controlling. I took that advice and it had completely turned our relationship around!

At one point in my personal development, I thought I had to teach others to do what I thought they should be doing. Later I learned to accept people the way they are. To change the world, you do not need to change others—you need to change yourself, work from within. When you make better choices for yourself, the world around you will change for the better. Move away from the things that keep you down: guilt, remorse, self-blame. Dwelling on them can never improve the situation. If you have past regrets, make sure they do not pass on to the present or the future. They will block your path and make it harder to get past them.

Remember that compassion is empowering. When you do good for others, the benefits will return to you many fold. If you want to be successful, help others achieve success and you will experience it too. After all, it is all up to *YOU.*

"Twenty years from now you will be more disappointed by the things that you didn't do than by the ones you did do. So throw off the bowlines. Sail away from the safe harbor. Catch the trade winds in your sails. Explore. Dream. Discover."
Mark Twain